GARDENING BYGONES

BOTANICAL GARDENS, REGENTS PARK, LONDON.

A Portrait in Old Picture Postcards

by

Malcolm Lumb

S.B. Publications

For my late father, John Albert Lumb

First published in 1996 by S.B.Publications
c/o 19 Grove Road, Seaford, East Sussex, BN25 1TP

ISBN 1 85770 107 0

Typeset by CGB Lewes

Printed and bound by MFP Design & Print
0161 864 4540

CONTENTS

CONTENTS

STAFF PORTRAITS

LAWNS AND PATHS

PLANTS UNDER GLASS

TOWN AND VILLAGE GARDENS

CONTENTS

CONTENTS

CONTENTS

ACKNOWLEDGEMENTS

THIS book is a tribute to all gardeners of the past who have dedicated their lives to the pursuit of garden excellence and to gardeners of the present who lavish all their energy and devotion, in true traditional style, on gardening in all its forms.

I am particularly indebted to those gardeners with whom I have had the opportunity to talk and for their help and information which has made this book a reality, and also to the people who have suggested that I should compile such a work. I should also like to thank Trevor and Maureen Haskard for their kindness in keying in the text.

All illustrations are from the author's own collection of postcards.

BIBLIOGRAPHY

Some suggested titles for readers seeking further information about nineteenth century horticultural practices:

The Traditional Garden Book by Graham Rose. Dorling Kindersley 1989
The Victorian Garden by Laurence Fleming and Allen Gore. Bell and Hyman 1984
Back to the Roots by Richard Mabey and Francesca Greenoak. Arrow Books 1983
Old Garden Tools by N Kay Sanecki. Shire Publications
Illustrated History of Gardening by A J Huxley. Paddington Press 1978

PLACES TO VISIT

It is advisable to check opening hours before setting out on a special journey

Kitchen Garden Museum, Clumber Park, Worksop, Notts. Tel: 01909 486411
British Lawn Mower Museum, 106–114 Shakespeare Street, Southport. Tel: 01704 535369
Northern Horticultural Society's Garden Museum, Harlow Carr Botanical Gardens, Craig Lane, Harrogate Tel: 01423 565418
The Tradescant Trust, Museum of Garden History, Lambeth Palace Road, London EC1
Henry Doubleday Research Association, National Centre for Organic Gardening, Ryton-on-Dunsmore, Coventry, Warwickshire. Tel: 01203 303517
The Museum of North Devon at Barnstaple has a collection of fern related items.

INTRODUCTION

How did their gardens grow?

MUCH has been written on the subject of horticulture. Virtually every conceivable aspect has been covered from the lavish extravagance of the gardens designed and laid out for stately homes by such geniuses as Capability Brown and Joseph Paxton through to the specialised cultivation of the Laced Dianthus – a flower brought to perfection by the Paisley weavers in the eighteenth century.

Throughout history no other pursuit has had more ardent students than horticulture. Gardening gives every person the opportunity to express his or her own concept of paradise irrespective of social standing. Indeed, in the nineteenth century it was in the garden where the master of the house and his outside staff could rub shoulders, all sense of status temporarily suspended, as they talked of prize-winning chrysanthemums and who had grown the most perfect leek.

To satisfy the seemingly inexhaustible appetite of those eager to create their own personal Garden of Eden a vast amount of specialist literature was produced from the middle of the nineteenth century. There were some excellent gardening journals, among them *The Horticultural Times,* a weekly paper costing sixpence. The *Gardeners' Chronicle,* priced at threepence in 1888, carried many advertisements for tools and young plants and was regarded as the gardeners' market place. Another magazine, *The Garden,* in 1877 offered its readers the 'Hundred Guinea Conservatory' and posed the following question from a subscriber: 'What are the best means of removing stains on flagstone in the greenhouse caused by falling flowers being trodden on?' Such was the intensity with which the Victorians pursued their interest.

Layout and the choice of plants was an individual affair with many influences affecting the final decision – none more so than that of fashion, particularly with regard to the planting of pleasure gardens. In the second half of the last century many fine shrubberies and herbaceous borders were replaced by rows upon rows of bedding plants. Geraniums, verbena and marigolds were popular with those affected by the 'bedding craze' and dazzled the eye with their garish colours.

Today it is only necessary to consult one of the many excellent books on garden design and planting in order to focus one's interest in a specific direction. The same could not be said a hundred years ago. Gardening was then more of a necessity for most of the population who needed to grow vegetables and herbs to supplement their incomes and feed their families.

True cottage gardens were a patchwork quilt of random informality. Chives grew alongside roses, hyssop with cabbage, carrots with sage. Only later was the practicality of this type of gardening appreciated for it was eventually noticed that herbs had a beneficial effect when planted among flowers and vegetables, repelling blackfly and mildew.

The choice and abundance of fruit and vegetables, coupled with their comparatively low cost, ease of cultivation and culinary excellence, ensured that most gardens sported at least a few varieties. The epicure was confronted with a wide choice, for seed catalogues in those days could contain as many as ten pages of, say, pea varieties alone.

Today the picture is very different. Choice is now dictated by EU rules and regulations with the emphasis on uniformity of shape, colour and size. Gone are many of the varieties known and affectionately pampered by gardeners of the past. The Carlin pea, its purple flowers a common sight in Elizabethan gardens, is no more. Bloody Warrior, with its non-conforming red splashed leaves, has fought its final battle and the brown and red Soldier bean, so called because of the fusilier soldier marking on the seed, has also become a casualty.

Fruit, too, has seen a decline – but for different reasons. It started in the 1600s with the rampant march of the Great Plague which took its toll of the experienced gardeners who carefully nurtured such ancient apple varieties as Roxberry Russet, Five Crowns and Catshead. Now orchards are being grubbed up, as have been many native hedgerows, and the orchardist is virtually an endangered species for commercial viability has restricted the choice of available fruits. However there are still 6,000 varieties of apple on the books of the National Apple Register and it rests with the gardeners of the 1990s to perpetuate for future generations the many ancient types that are still available.

What of the gardeners of yesterday? What specialist equipment did they have to protect the blooms of carnations from rain and too much sun? How were fruit and vegetables cultivated to exhibition standard? What was needed to support melons as they hung precariously from wooden struts? How were cucumbers persuaded to grow straight?

It was not until the end of the last century that tool and equipment manufacturers began to produce what was necessary to deal with these problems. Previously it was common practice for gardeners to get the implements they wanted for specific jobs made for them by the village blacksmith.

These hand forged tools have a uniqueness and charm that is immediately evident when they are held in the hand. The hammered indentations on the metal reflect the skill and accuracy of the smith and his pride in a job well done. The wooden shaft is often hand cut, and socketed to the metal end instead of being strapped on. The initials of the owner are often burnt into the handle.

The tool could have belonged to a suburban enthusiast toiling on his small plot or to an in-service gardener whose profession was an art and a craft which demanded perfection in every detail. Members of this elite workforce were skilled at everything from keeping temperature constant in sub-tropical hot houses to knowing by touch when a melon was ready for picking.

The layout of the gardens they tended would be determined by the size of the house. Generally at least an acre, surrounded by ten foot high walls, would be devoted to edible vegetation for the master's table. The vegetables would be grown in regimented rows in beds edged with box and tended by an army of craftsmen under the direction of the bowler-hatted head gardener.

Shows gave head gardeners an opportunity to display their choicest and zealously prized specimens and meet and compete with their peers. There were many specialist shows catering for a single type of fruit or vegetable and each would have a dedicated following. Take the gooseberry, for instance. On the show benches the choicest berries were housed in purpose built cases, each of which held an average of fifty gooseberries. The fruits were weighed with small brass weights, often as flat as a square of paper, and known as a penny-weight. The winning berry would be placed at the very top of a sloping tray with the runners up in trays underneath.

There are few shows of this sort left today. Gardening has been brought into line with contemporary living. Bio-degradable pots have replaced the hand made terracotta pots and conservatories have become terranium – all to reduce time and labour, with cost being the single significant factor in the decline in the number of garden staff employed.

Having grown old fashioned varieties of plants for a number of years and collected tools and equipment for a similar period, it was a natural progression for me to collect illustrations of gardeners with the tools of their trade. These illustrations, which form the basis of this book, cover many different styles of gardening and also deal with a subject that has had scant mention in the past – the actual gardener.

Malcolm F Lumb
Loscoe, Derbyshire

PERGOLA FROM KITCHEN GARDENS MANOR

THE WALLED KITCHEN GARDEN was always situated a respectable distance from the house and its practical appearance screened from visitors to the pleasure grounds. The high walls were a defence against rabbits which, given the chance, could devastate crops. They were also a deterrent to the two legged opportunist thief eager for free produce and provided a surface against which to train fruit trees.

Part of the Kitchen Gardens

A TRADITIONAL LAYOUT showing produce for the big house growing in box edged beds separated by gravel walks and surrounded by walls adorned with varieties of fan trained fruit trees. The average kitchen garden measured 230 feet by 150 feet and as many as fifty gardeners would be employed in its cultivation. The head gardener would have his own living quarters – the under gardeners and foremen housed together in a 'bothy'.

BOTHY STAFF *c* **1900.** Their garb was rough and thick and always topped off with a waistcoat and tie. The foreman, on the left, wears an apron to denote his position in the garden hierarchy. Flat caps were worn by all but head gardeners – who sported bowler hats. A fine of threepence, or even sixpence in some establishments, would be levied upon a gardener who turned up for work on a Monday morning wearing a dirty shirt.

THE GARDENS, SANDRINGHAM. Much of the work in the grander establishments was of a temporary nature, lasting only as long as it took to produce a crop or pick the produce. Jobbing gardeners travelled around the country in search of seasonal work and to help them obtain it many of them belonged to a benevolent order of gardeners, the trade make of which was a scar on the arm made by a pruning knife.

COPPED HALL, MIDDLESEX, *c* **1908,** with a fine array of the glasshouses which allowed the Victorians to cultivate such exotics as pineapples, figs and nectarines. The size of a house depended on seasonal crop requirements and ventilation was controlled by hand-operated opening lights. Shade was provided by covering the panes with thatched mats or painting them with a proprietary brand of shading such as Summer Cloud.

A Corner of Kitchen Gardens

GROSVENOR SANATORIUM, KENNINGTON, ASHFORD, KENT in springtime – the start of the gardening year when soil preparation is of prime importance. The two estate gardeners pictured would have been assigned the task of cultivation and sowing the seeds once the beds had been prepared. Another job for this time of the year was tying in and spraying the fruit trees trained against the walls.

IN FULL PRODUCTION. The head gardener stands in the door of one of the glasshouses proudly surveying his kingdom. He had to be fairly ingenious with his methods of cultivation as often at short notice he would be called upon to supply exhibition vegetables and exotic fruits for the table. He raised them with the aid of frames, hotbeds and pots, using the experience and the expertise which earned him a salary equal to that of the butler.

GROUND MANAGEMENT in progress, with the head gardener looking at the camera while his under gardeners are busy with their appointed tasks. Formality was a predominant feature of gardens of this type. Landscape artists were sometimes called upon to create a natural look which they achieved with a combination of lawns, vistas and gravel walkways among a copious planting of trees.

WEEDING THE BEDS has always been a tedious but necesary task. Here the lady of the house is doing the chore by hand but there were purpose made devices for getting rid of the weeds – everything, in fact, from small grubbers to slender brass and copper tubes containing noxious poisons which were injected into the stem of the plant. This was a method favoured by head gardeners when labour was required on more important jobs.

BEDDING OUT was much in fashion towards the latter half of the last century. Head gardeners would be instructed to raise sufficient seed from annual plants to fill existing beds, or to create new ones. Some of the grander schemes featured island beds linked together in intricate geometrical patterns and containing upwards of 100,000 young plants. Popular for such harmonious displays of colour were geraniums, salvia, verbena and lobelia.

SPRING AND SUMMER DISPLAYS in herbaceous borders and island beds were almost as labour intensive as the kitchen garden. No sooner was the welcome splash of colour provided by daffodils and tulips over than room had to be made for semi-permanent displays of many varieties of geranium. The most popular for massed displays was the dwarf, Tom Thumb. By the turn of the century variegated leaved varieties had been developed.

TYING IN CHRYSANTHEMUMS with raffia to rigid canes helped the plants grow upright and sturdy for display purposes. To finish off they were potted up in containers which were placed on bricks to ensure good drainage. In hot weather a gardener was assigned to check the pots to see if the plants needed watering, and did so by tapping the pot with a cane. If it rang when hit it was a sure sign that water was needed.

PLANTS IN CONTAINERS have always been in fashion. Over the years many types of container have been used, from terra cotta pots to elaborate stoneware troughs. A turn of the century favourite, much used today, was a sawn-in-half wooden barrel. It provided the perfect receptacle for half hardy annuals as the wood allowed them to breathe and at the same time it was water retentive.

A ROSE WALK, with many varieties arranged in straight lines and suitable colour combinations, was a feature of the gardens of many large villas. Gardeners allocated to the care of roses had to be adept at layering and pruning. Suckers were a continual problem – the attendant gardener having to distinguish between a growth-reducing spur and a healthy shoot. Growth was promoted by a high potassium feed in spring and autumn.

THE POTTING SHED, in the vicinity of which these two apprentices were pictured in 1910, was in the grounds of 7 Conway Place, Hove, a large seaside villa long since demolished. A bus station was built on its foundations and still stands today as the headquarters of the Brighton and Hove Bus and Coach Company. The pots necessary for planting up had to be cleaned and stacked in rows within wooden frames.

WATERING THE GARDEN to produce lush vegetation and a profusion of blooms in herbaceous borders could occupy as many as ten men at a time. Special water engines and carts were used such as the Barnes patent water cart seen at the top of the path. These cylindrical containers had a spray attachment operated by a hand pump and were mounted on wheels so they could be moved easily to drought affected areas.

THE SUNDIAL, unlike so many garden ornaments, had a practical purpose. The hours of the day could be determined by the shadows cast by the sun upon its brass faced dial. This functional aid had therefore to be placed in the open where the sun's rays could reach it from rising to setting. It was also a decorative item and often used to provide a focal point on lawns or, as this picture shows, in formal rose gardens.

Love in a Garden.

LOVE IN A GARDEN is the title of this card by James Henderson and Sons. The staff appear to be overwhelmed by the feminine charms of the lady of the house. She, in addition to her usual duties, would on occasions inspect the garden to see that work there was progressing smoothly and would have her say in plantings or particular arrangements, especially if the master was otherwise engaged.

PREPARING FOOD in the kitchen of a country house in Worcestershire. The head cook, after receiving instructions about the menu, which would be drawn up daily, would inform the head gardener, via the garden boy, of what fruit and vegetables would be required that day. The meal would be prepared in regimental style, each member of the kitchen staff having his or her duties dictated by the cook.

AN UNEASY ALLIANCE existed between indoor and outdoor staff as this picture shows. The cook, centre, was not renowned for her tolerance and would make unreasonable demands, often at short notice, for out-of-season fruit and vegetables. Her attendant maids were given short thrift if they were not always hard at work. The garden staff can be identified by the tools they carry – the man on the right has a fine scythe and sharpening stone.

GARDEN STAFF, ROTHBURY, NORTHUMBERLAND. At the time these gardeners were pictured the average wage for a first class foreman was twenty five shillings a week. Herbaceous borders required the undivided attention of at least three full time gardeners in weeding, deadheading, spraying and staking. It was not until the manpower shortage that followed the First World War that wages began to rise and gardening styles change.

AMONG THE FRAMES

·STANDING proudly among the frames, having just watered the plants they contain, is this young glasshouse man. It was his responsibility to start off, and bring on, crops ready for picking in advance of those grown outside.

The frames were always in close proximity to the greenhouses so plants could be easily transferred from one to the other. Their brick built bases were topped by wooden frames and glass lights. These could be moved up or down to provide the right amount of ventilation needed in the weather conditions at the time.

It was not uncommon for large gardens to have in excess of twenty of these frames for successive sowings.

THE FERN GARDEN was much loved by the Victorians and they organised fern hunts in the hope of discovering a new variety or different leaf form. Specimens were kept indoors in glass and metal Wardian cases and outside the spore laden rhizomes were grown in stone grottoes. Here the staff are resting from the backbreaking task of weeding the fernery – a job done with the special canes held by the man on the right.

THE WILDERNESS GARDEN. Planting or re-positioning large trees and shrubs around the grounds was a cumbersome and time consuming task occupying a fair number of gardeners. Trees presented the greatest challenge when an instant garden was required. Special wagons which resembled open railway wagons, were used to tranport young trees, complete with root ball, to the site. They would be winched into position by horse power.

ALL IN A DAY'S WORK

THE delights of gardening – with lovely scenery, a pretty girl in a pretty dress holding a besom broom and leaning on the handle of an elaborately decorated roller.

The roller in the picture is The Sandringham, one of the models made in Leicester by a firm which produced many fine and ornately embellished rollers for use in the garden.

It also made land rollers for use on cricket fields and the lawns of large estates. They were made of cast iron and the drums filled with sand or water to achieve the necessary weight.

Earlier rollers were cumbersome things to move about, the drums being of solid stone.

CLEARING AWAY THE LEAVES

FROM autumn through to the spring fallen leaves on drives and paths presented visitors to the house with a slippery prospect.

To be sure there were no accidents and that anyone calling at the house did not get his or her shoes muddied, two of the garden boys would be delegated to the job of path maintenance.

Armed with a wheelbarrow, besom broom, shovel and a bucket they had the daily task of collecting the fallen leaves and transferring them to the compost heap.

THE YOUNG APPRENTICE

IT was general practice for a youth to be apprenticed as a gardener at the age of sixteen, prior to which he would have served as a garden boy

After four years as an apprentice he would be qualified as a journeyman and be able to widen his horticultural knowledge by working on all aspects of cultivation and maintenance on an estate or garden, eventually becoming a foreman.

Hinxton Hall. Cambs. West views

HORSE POWER was essential to achieve the striped, closely cut lawns which graced the gardens of many a stately home. The Green's wheel geared mower in use here had a forty two inch cut. As the turf could be damaged by a horse's hooves they were covered by leather boots which came in two sizes – one for ponies, the other for horses. Two gardeners looked after the mowing, one guiding the machine, the other leading the horse.

MOWING AT LEONARDSLEE. Two in service gardeners at work on the lawns of the Loder family's large estate in Sussex. The cumbersome machine they are using is made of cast iron and has a thirty six inch cut. It appears to be a special occasion as the horse is sporting bells and brasses on its harness and the leather boots on its hooves are highly polished. Or was all the spit and polish just for the photograph?

RANSOME'S GRASS CUTTER. The chain driven mower was a Victorian invention and introduced around 1895. It started the standardisation of the lawn mower and, as if to advertise its purpose, came in an overall green colour which could vary in tone from dark to light, depending on the batch from the production line. This type of machine was produced until 1931, with little appreciable change in appearance or performance.

GREEN'S LAWN MOWERS ENSURE A PERFECT LAWN AND ARE A PLEASURE TO USE
OBTAINABLE OF THE BEST IRONMONGERS AND SEEDSMEN

GREEN'S LAWN MOWERS. This large lawn mower company had works in Leeds and London and was able to offer the discerning gardener a wide choice of cutting machinery. Mowers of all types and to suit all pockets were available, from the eight inch Silens Messor costing £6 through to the forty two inch Green's patent motor mower, which in 1923 would have cost £340 – then the price of an average house.

TIME FOR A SERVICE. As with anything mechanical, lawn mowers required servicing and repairing. Blades needed to be sharpened and the drive key within the hub could go astray and have to be replaced. Although the design was simple the machines could sustain damage in inexperienced hands, particularly the early cast iron models. A complete strip down and service by a knowledgeable dealer would take two days.

LEAN-TO GREENHOUSES were the most popular form of glass, brick and iron structures. They made it possible for anyone with a sizeable amount of walled perimeter to have
a supply of out-of-season vegetables and exotic fruit all the year round. Additional houses
were built on as required for individual crops. Some specialist houses were given over com-
pletely to one particular cultivar such as peaches, roses or figs.

SUB TROPICAL SPLENDOUR.

THE Victorians and the Edwardians loved their heated conservatories in which they would grow tropical and sub tropical species.

Within these artificially created rain forests borders were planted up with as many different species as they could accommodate..

Palms held a particular fascination for the gardeners of yesterday and in order that the luxuriant growth could be enjoyed both day and night, huge gas-powered lamps were installed.

A WELL STOCKED GREENHOUSE

A turn of the century green-house with pots of geraniums lined up along the window struts and a further display at floor level, the whole set off by the tempting fruit of the black Hamburg vine.

Once it had fruited the vine would be put to bed for the winter. All the dead wood and unwanted shoots would be pruned out and the leaders lowered to floor level to allow the sap to build up for the following season.

FLOWER CULTURE

A YOUNG member of staff is holding a pot of lilies – perfect subjects for the unheated greenhouse as they are such hardy plants.

However, lilies hate being disturbed when in flower and the blooms had to be cut sparingly so the bulbs did not sustain too severe a shock.

Once dormant, the bulbs would be lifted and packed into special lily crates to build up their reserves of strength to produce next year's display of bloom.

CARNATION CULTURE. As no gentleman wished to be seen abroad without a carnation in his buttonhole it was the duty of his gardener to produce blooms worthy of this position. A temperature of 55° F was maintained in the greenhouse and the plants were never allowed to dry out at the roots. They received weekly applications of liquid soot and cow manure when in flower and any greenfly was removed individually with an aphid brush.

GETTING TO WORK

FRUIT picking was the time when the ladder got an airing in the smaller back gardens of town and village houses.

The whole family would make a day of it. Those able to climb the ladder, or the trees, would pick the fruit and pass it down to those standing underneath with baskets at the ready.

The crop was then taken into the house and stored, the day being rounded off with a picnic and games.

AMONG THE BEEHIVES at the bottom of the garden this Victorian family poses proudly for the camera. There were as many books on bees and their care as on gardening and hives came in all manner of shapes and sizes, the WBC or small cottage type being among the prettiest. They were always sited near a good supply of pollen, clover being the most popular choice among bee keepers – hence the saying 'in clover'.

WINTER SUN

'HOW'S this for winter time' is the comment written at the bottom of this card. The vest-clad Cornishman, dazzled by the winter sun, is cultivating produce that can, because of the climate in this region, be grown up to a month in advance of the rest of the country.

He is holding what has become known as a Cornish spade, and appears to be enjoying his spell of winter digging.

EAST ANGLIAN ENDEAVOUR

THE face of a seasoned gardener, if ever there was one, looks out from this post card from Potter Heigham, Norfolk.

The ridged semi circular spade with a D shaped handle that he is using is of a type much favoured in the Midlands and East Anglia.

In the south west gardeners seemed to have preferred the long handled Cornish spade and in the Home Counties they opted for the threaded spade. There was as much variation in handle designs as there was in digging ends.

A PICTURE OF CONTENTMENT

WHAT better way to pass the time in the garden than by having your photograph taken in a favourite spot which, for this gardener, is clearly his greenhouse.

Even when in the garden appearances had to be kept up. This gardener's attire is quite formal with, of course, collar and tie, a suitable old jacket and hat and perhaps a pair of clogs on the feet that are hidden by foliage.

RAISING PLANTS FROM SEED

THERE are many advantages to be gained from raising plants from seed as an alternative to buying them. In addition to the obvious factor of cost, there are other considerations.

If a variety is in short supply then its continuation is assured as long as the seeds are kept in cool, dry conditions.

There is also the additional bonus of knowing the variety being sown is disease free and will not introduce clubroot or other soil based diseases.

'MORE PEGS, MUM?' A character who could relate many a gardening yarn is pictured in the process of making clothes pegs. He is using two pruning knives and a hammer with the claw end of which he would make the initial split in a round piece of wood. After fashioning the peg to the desired shape one of the pruning knives is inserted and progressively nudged further up the split while the other is used to widen and make the V end.

NATURE'S GARLAND is everywhere in this picture of a woodman's cottage. It was the practice, in many instances, to cover a place of abode with some sort of lush foliage, either as an extension of the garden or to improve upon or complement the appearance of the facade. This cottage is bedecked with native ivy and in the garden there is a hotchpotch planting of chrysanthemums, foxgloves and pinks.

A DAY OUT FOR THE FAMILY, before transport became cheaply available for the majority, often took the form of some combined activity in the garden. Father would direct operations, under the watchful eye of mother. In this long garden, typical of many turn of the century terraced cottages, there are flowers on one side of the central path and vegetables in abundance on the other. An old tin bath is being used as a temporary plant container.

PLANTS IN PLENTY. It is to gardens like this than many of the plants taken for granted today owe their continued existence. If father, seen here resting from his labours while his wife picks some flowers for the house, had opted for a maintenance free layout of conifers and hybridised plants, this picture of profusion would not have been taken and many lovely varieties would have been lost to future generations.

FAN TRAINED TREES grace the facade of this thatched cottage in the Cotswolds. Although they look attractive espaliered trees need a lot of maintenance to give a good account of themselves. The central stem has to be lopped off at the right height and laterals carefully selected, with only the strongest used as a leader and secured to the stone with harpoon shaped iron clasps over protective strips of hessian.

A TRADITIONAL COTTAGE GARDEN with vegetables and flowers growing side by side in carefree and happy communion. The older vegetable varieties produce just as much colour in the garden as their non-edible counterparts. Purple flowering peas and yellow and red flowering beans cheerfully complement pink mallows, red lynchnis and purple toadflax.

PROSPECT HOUSE has its typically northern granite-faced facade embellished with an unusual grotto-style opening leading to the rear of the property. The gardener is using a traditional lawn rake to clear away the leaves of autumn. Rakes of this type were once in general use but are rarely seen nowadays. There is no obvious reason for their disappearance unless today there is less time available for grooming the lawn.

PLANTING OUT. The gardener is using a dibber to put in some seedlings, guarded by his trusty companion. The dibber has the D shaped handle typical of ones used in the Midlands and either a plain pointed wooden end or one made of steel. Among other varieties of dibber were ones with elaborately turned handles, the iron and steel plumbobs used in kitchen gardens and the simple ash bobbin types favoured by nurserymen.

PLANT PROTECTION. Small round saucer shaped discs were introduced by the carnation growing weavers in the Paisley area to protect their show blooms from too much sun or splashes of rain. The discs, which became known as calyx shades, were in fact oiled paper cups supported by special pins. When a profusion of these shades was seen in a garden it was a sure sign that the owner was aiming for show success.

WALSOKEN RECTORY, NORFOLK, showing the box-edged beds which reached the height of their popularity in Victorian times. The small evergreen shrubs were planted at four inch intervals and kept at the desired height by spring and autumn clipping. Propagation was by sub-division which was just as well as up to thirty plants were needed to surround an island bed and each one could cost as much as a flowering perennial.

This is a Wood.

This is Miss Spencer.

This is a maid with Spade + Sac[k]

And this is a heap of Leaf Mould

Clear th[...] a bad[...] gard[...]

This is the tenant of said garden

'IF YOU GO DOWN TO THE WOODS TODAY'

THIS pen and ink card shows the lady of the house, accompanied by her maid armed with a spade and a sack, off to the woods to collect fallen leaves.

Leaf mould compost has always been valued for its ability to enrich and aerate the soil, thus allowing nutrients to penetrate and promote healthy growth.

It is also a good medium, for taming heavy and clay loams. To give of its best the leaves have to be gathered together in a heap in the fall and then used the following spring after microbes and worms have broken them down.

WILLING HANDS were the most cost effective means of tilling, weeding and cultivating the soil to produce good crops. Tractors and other mechanical aids were considered by those who had taken vows of poverty to be expensive luxuries. Although the work was hard, starting at dawn and not finishing until dusk, the many casual workers employed in the monasteries were grateful for a wholesome meal and a roof over their heads.

CLOSE KNIT COMMUNITIES

RELIGIOUS orders each had their own doctrines, with an underlying bond of community spirit. Here members pose for the camera armed with the appropriate tools for the tasks they are about to undertake.

The summer house in the background is typical of such·buildings in the Victorian period. It would have side supports made from conifers, a porch of larch and walls of rustic wovenwork

Although the basic design varied little over the years it became fashionable to create structures of more and more elaborate rusticity..

East Side, S. MARY'S CONVENT, CHISWICK

ST MARY'S CONVENT, CHISWICK with a gardener preparing an island bed for a display of red geraniums. Many of the plants were grown principally for their practical use and others for their biblical significance, arrangements perhaps taking the form of a cross or floral cloister. Some beds would be dedicated to a particular saint and the plants in them carefully chosen for their connection with him or her.

COURTYARD GARDENING

THE warm climate in the Mediterranean area is ideal for growing olives and citrus fruits in stone pots. The scene portrayed is typical of this form of cultivation in monasteries in Italy.

Citrus fruits like these lemons do not take kindly to being grown in direct sunlight. Their principal requirement is a moist root run and to make sure they had water where and when it was needed special iron bars were used to probe the bottom of the pots and holes bored in the roots through which water was added.

GARDENERS AT WORK. MOUNT SAINT BERNARD'S ABBEY.

MOUNT ST BERNARD'S ABBEY. Providing food for the fraternity was delegated to those who showed an aptitude for the work. A small group headed by a monk gardener was in overall charge of a garden made up of small sections. Vegetables were grown in walled or wattle fenced enclosures with the glasshouses and fruit gardens nearby. Here five pronged forks are being used, instead of the more usual four pronged ones.

Dunster, Dovecot and Old Priory

DUNSTER DOVECOT. Keeping pigeons was another form of supplementing the food supply. Hundreds of years ago many fine stone structures, like this one at the old priory at Dunster, were built for the purpose of breeding, rearing and culling these birds for the table. There was the added bonus of a constant supply of eggs and the birds' droppings made an excellent manure for the garden.

THE HERBARIUM, KEW. It is only at establishments like these that plants from all over the world can be examined and studied. The Herbarium has the largest collection of dried plants in existence. Stored within a labyrinth of purpose-built display cabinets and drawers are some three million specimens representing the existing flora of the whole world as well as some that have sadly become extinct.

THE POTTING SHED ... ...TICULTURAL COLLEGE FOR WOMEN

A CENTRE OF LEARNING. There is a lot of activity taking place in the potting shed of this horticultural college for women, the name of which has faded from the photograph. The containerised plants are being moved by hand cart to their destination while the work of potting up continues on the benches. The compost piled up in the foreground would have consisted of a mixture of loam, ash and ground up broken crockery.

READY FOR INSPECTION. These young gardeners lined up for the camera with their allotted tools, are about to be instructed on the basics of gardening before moving on to work as garden boys on large estates. Even at this lowly stage in their chosen career the boys were expected to show a flair for gardening work in general. It was up to the foreman to give the novice gardeners jobs for which they showed an aptitude.

PEACH HOUSE at Wannock Gardens, Polegate, Sussex. To grow peaches successfully it is essential to maintain a constant temperature of 50° F in the glasshouse in the winter months and to supply ample ventilation. Gardeners under training would be shown how to pollinate the trees by dusting the flowers over at noon with a rabbit's foot mounted on a stick and how to deal with attacks of red mite and peach leaf curl.

STARTING EARLY

THIS young lass proudly poses with her watering can by the tomato plants. These were often grown in pails and terra cotta pots, nurserymen using a thirteen inch diameter pot in which they would put three tomato plants.

The advantage of raising tomatoes in containers was that they could be moved round the garden to obtain the maximum sunlight.

EXCHANGING TIPS. Handy tips can be picked up when gardeners get together. Here there is a simple but effective earwig trap formed by the upturned plants pots seen in the foreground. The pots were filled with straw and placed on sticks. The earwigs, looking for a dry and comfortable resting place, would climb up the sticks and settle in the straw. The gardener would then remove them, straw and all, and dispose of them.

THE CABBAGE CROP. This Midlands allotment holder, his D handled spade denoting the area in which this photograph was taken, has obviously been giving his brassicas the nitrogen they need for successful cultivation. He would also have had tbeen keeping a watchful eye out for this vegetable's main predator, the Cabbage White butterfly. If left unchecked the caterpillars of this pretty creature can decimate a crop.

DIGGING FOR VICTORY

PROPAGANDA card No 513 demonstrates how everybody could do their bit for the war effort. All gardeners were called upon to their level best to beat the U boats and feed the nation.

It was the Second World War that put an end to the traditional manor house type of garden. On the Home Front flower beds were planted with culinary herbs, many ornamental hedges were grubbed out to give extra space for cultivation and luxury items such as peaches, raspberries and cardoons were replaced by rows and rows of nutritious potatoes.

A NURSERY IN HOLLAND with a group of workers tying in the developing young plants with raffia. This job was cost effective for the owners only because of the comparative pittance paid to the labour force. Most of them were itinerant, travelling many miles staking tomatoes, pruning grapes and picking fruit as the season demanded. The accommodation with which they were provided was basic – often just beds of hessian in open sheds.

SECURING THE CROP. It was standard practice to grow cucumbers and melons together as each initally required the same conditions. Only when the fruit began to ripen did a different aftercare become necessary. As the melons started to swell their weight had to be supported and at first boxes were used for this purpose. Later they were replaced by specially made cotton nets which cost three shillings a dozen.

FRUIT SPRAYING. Trials of new equipment and sprays were carried out during the dormant season – the ideal time to stop destructive pests such as the mealy bug and red spider mite from mutilating the summer crops. These insects laid eggs in the upper branches of the fruit trees in winter, their offspring burrowing into the young fruit in the spring. The machine in the picture is a Barnes patent water and garden engine.

WINTER PRUNING. If left to its own devices this fruit tree would grow prolifically with a resulting over-abundance of random top growth. The nurseryman is pruning it back in order that its branches do not rub against each other, damaging the bark and so allowing infection to set in. Too much growth has the added disadvantage of restricting air circulation and reducing the amount of light needed by the developing fruit.

The Long House, Longfield Vinery, Guernsey.
750 ft. long, crop averaging 25,000 bunches of Grapes.

LONGFIELD VINERY, GUERNSEY. There were nearly forty different varieties of vines producing fruit for culinary use in Britain at the turn of the century, the Black Hamburg being the most popular. When cut the grapes, with stems attached, were kept fresh by putting them in long flat bottomed glass bottles with upward tapering necks. Water was added through a hole at the top of the bottle and drawn up through the stem to the fruit.

FRUIT PICKERS

WOMEN as well as men were employed to pick the ripening crops as this photograph of a group from the Evesham area shows.

Most of the workforce was migratory and provision had to be made for their accommodation by the landowner.

Each worker was issued with a numbered tally to ensure that only those actually engaged for the work were lodged and fed.

SWEET PEAS have always been a popular cultivar, both for their scent when indoors and as an exhibition flower. Wem in Shropshire is considerd to be the home of the plant. A one time head gardener, Henry Eckford, set up a sweet pea nursery there and it still has one of the premier shows in the country, with more than fifty sweet pea classes. Many of the shops are specially decorated for the occasion.

EXHIBITION FRUIT

HOW about these for gooseberries? They have been trained as single stem cordons and carefully nurtured to the highest standard for exhibition at a local show.

The protective sheet behind the plants acted as a windbreak and, because it was white, doubled up as a suntrap, retaining the warmth collected during the day and releasing it at night.

As large fruits were required for show purposes the foliage was kept to a minimum.

AN ONION PATCH with a splendid display of exhibition quality plants. Onions prefer a dry mellow sub soil and, if possible, to be grown in the same bed each year. A nineteenth century writer, advising on the growing of onions, said: `If the soil should be exhausted recruit it with a compost of fresh loam and rotten dung, avoiding to use stable dung in a rank, reduced state'.

DAHLIAS ON DISPLAY. As with chrysanthemums, with which they share similar growing conditions, dahlias look their best when in a mass. The plant is of Swedish origin, named after Andreas Dahl. It reached England around 1840 and attracted an immediate cult following, especially with cottage gardners who planted it in beds. Florists found the flowers appealing and arranged cacti dahlias in special wire bloom holders.

SUDBURY PARK HOTEL. Here there are many decorative features, the focal point being a vase on a pedestal. The hedging portrays various animals and provides an interesting vista. There are many types of topiary for the connoisseur including mazes, knots and architectural subjects. The most time consuming to maintain are figures for they require elaborate steel structures to give access to unwanted new buds in inaccessible parts.

A SUB TROPICAL FERN HOUSE

THE conservatory entrance to W C Hollands Horticultural Establishment with a fine display of sphagnum covered containers hanging from the roof and some impressive specimens of fern trees and palms.

High humidity was the key to success in this type of environment. A spray system was developed which had a timing device which could be pre-set to ensure the sprays came on at the required intervals, thus ensuring the well being of the moisture loving plants.

CLASSIC DECORATION. Another decorative feature in the grounds of Sudbury Park Hotel is this classic Empire style sundial with winged and standing figures. Although no longer required for the purpose of marking the passage of time sundials are objects of interest in a garden. The great eighteenth century garden designers would use them to act as focal points at the end of a vista or within the rose garden.

THE PERGOLA, SANDRINGHAM. This impressive structure follows the simple layout inroduced by notable landscape architects around the turn of the century. Although the design rarely varied many different materials were used. Cottage gardeners usually opted for an intricate display of rustic trellis work and the owners of larger houses would choose pagoda like structures covered with climbers.

AN APPLE ARCH in the gardens of Myton Hall in Warwickshire. The shape was formed by planting rows of trees approximately five feet apart. The outgrowing branches were kept at roughly the same height as those of the neighbouring tree. Fruiting spurs were formed by cutting back the laterals by three inches and the resulting growth by one and a half inches. The tips of the trees were tied together and the whole attached to a metal framework.

UNIVERSAL FLOWER SHOW, GHENT

BEAUTY and blooms combine on this coloured postcard to attract everyone interested in horticulture to a show staged in Belgium in April 1913.

The event was hailed as the most successful staging of European horticulture. There were thousands of stalls all competing for orders from representatives of city corporations and other civic organisations who were there to see the latest in garden design and planting schemes.

MAIDSTONE HORTICULTURAL SHOW. Here is all the atmosphere of a turn of the century English country show with bunting and candle powered lanterns in abundance. A good cross section of the community is represented and, as was customary, flowers and produce are arranged on trestle tables on opposite sides of the marquee. Note the sloping wooden cabinets for displaying various types of flowers.

HYACINTH SHOW at Wombwell in Yorkshire. Many specialised shows had their origins firmly in the central and northern parts of the country. The qualities the judges looked for were the form of flowers, colour and leaf formation. Hyacinths were very much a florist's flower and, according to horticultural journals of the day, some 1,800 different varieties existed in the 1870s, including Double Yellows and Blues.

EXHIBITION BLOOMS. Foremost among the specialised shows were the ones dedicated to the chrysanthemum. The four main features on which it was judged were form, size, freshness and colour. To show off the flowers to their best coloured clothes were placed behind the banked vases of blooms. The aim was to show a large collection of good heads rather than a few blooms of exhibition quality.

A FLORIST'S DISPLAY. There were almost as many specialist containers used for show purposes as there were flowers to put in them. These chrysanthemums are in brightly decorated glass or stone containers with long necks. At the Wakefield Tulip Show the stalk of a specimen bloom was inserted through a hole in the lid of a tall stone jar. Carnation fanciers used metal containers with tapered necks.

SKINNER AND JOHNSON supplied customers with a comprehensive illustrated listing of tools for the gardener which they made at their works just west of Gainsborough. As can be seen from the display many of the tools were used in both agriculture and horticulture. These two forms of cultivation went hand in hand in market gardens, nurseries and orchards.

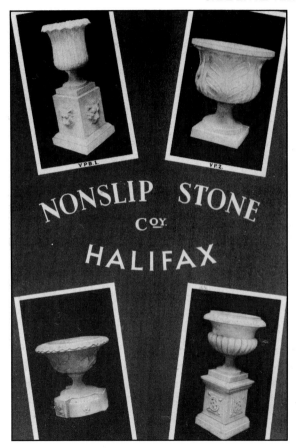

GARDEN STATUARY

TRADITIONALLY garden ornaments took the form of decorated stone urns and vases, classic figures and heraldic beasts.

Care was taken with those containing plants that the flowers and foliage did not hide the elegant lines or artistic details of the container.

As stone was very expensive it was considered good garden practice to bring any statuary indoors for the winter or, if this was not practical, to protect them against frost with some form of covering.

PULHAM AND SON was one of the leading landscape gardening specialists of the nineteenth century and the firm's artificially textured stone was much in demand for natural looking rock formations. At Madresfield in Worcestershire they created a natural fernery so expertly that it was impossible to tell the artificial rocks from the real thing without the very closest examination.

FLORAL FACADE

THIS Victorian posy shop has all its floral offerings lovingly arranged to show them off to the very best advantage.

Hours of work must have gone into creating this daily display.

Today, unfortunately, there are not many individualist shops like this one in the High streets of even the older market towns,

J. C. WHEELER & SON'S STAND ROYAL SHOW, 1909, ON WHICH OCCASION HIS MAJESTY VISITED GLOUCESTER.

WELL PHOTO CO.   MANCHES

ROYAL SHOW STAND. Wheeler and Son of Gloucester had a lavish display at the 1909 Royal Show when King Edward VII visited Gloucester, as can be seen from this acknowledgement card sent out to customers. Wheeler's was one of the larger seed firms and produced a profusely illustrated catalogue of the diverse species it could supply to growers – everything from vegetables to exotic flowers and fruits for the greenhouse.

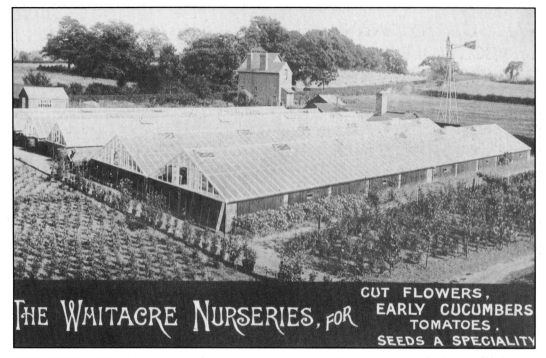

THE WHITACRE NURSERIES, FOR CUT FLOWERS, EARLY CUCUMBERS TOMATOES, SEEDS A SPECIALITY

NURSERY CARD. An acknowledgement card from Whiteacre Nurseries informing the recipient of the time, date and place his or her esteemed order would be delivered. These trade cards are among the most colourful and descriptive of all postcards relating to gardens and gardening, featuring as they do the specialities of the particular establishment and details of trophies won and awards gained.

WEBBS' SPRING CATALOGUE
OF VEGETABLE AND FLOWER SEEDS, etc.

Published annually in January.

PRICE 1s.
POST FREE.

Allowed off subsequent orders.

GRATIS TO CUSTOMERS.

Contains complete cultural instructions and lists, Illustrations, etc. of the Newest and Best

**VEGETABLES,
FLOWERS,
POTATOES,**
etc., etc.

WEBB & SONS
The King's Seedsmen
WORDSLEY,
STOURBRIDGE.

CATALOGUE CARD. Edwardian gardeners are invited by Webb and Sons – the King's Seedsmen, please note – to order the firm's spring catalogue. These catalogue were as plentiful then as they are now but surprisingly few old ones have survived to give an insight into what was available in earlier days. Many catalogues listed a huge number of different varieties of just one seed type.

THE LITTLE GRIPPER

TO help with gathering fruit long handled secateurs were introduced to give access to the upper branches.

The Little Gripper was one such device. It was advertised as 'suitable for ladies' because of its light weight and it could also be used to 'weed without stooping'.

On the reverse of this card, which is addressed to the manufacturers, is a hand written on approval request for the Little Gripper garden tool.

All the customer had to do was fill in his or her name and address where indicated and agree to either return the tool within three days or send a five shilling postal order (or seven shillings and sixpence for the 'Edition de Luxe')

HOMESPUN YARN

AN advertising card from one of the large seed companies in existence in 1906.

The firm's name is not on the reverse but its address is given as 9,10,11, Addle Street, London, EC and printed below it is the caption to the photograph which reads:

Cotton grown at Marl House, Bexley, ENGLAND by Sir Robert H Rogers, from Seed imported from SOUTH AFRICA.

In order to sell their seeds firms made many claims about the superiority of them – improved, selected or advanced being favourite descriptions.

TOOLS OF THE TRADE

WHEN standardisation crept in to the production of garden tools there remained plenty of customers who wanted something special and manufacturers and retailers only too happy to supply them.

Such a purveyor of tools was William Hunt and Sons of The Brades, Birmingham who chose this jolly looking white bearded old countryman to get across the message that 'good gardeners use only Brades Brand'.

Manufacturers produced catalogues listings many different types of spades, forks and hoes. A typical toolsman's catalogue of as little as seventy years ago would list twenty different types of fork alone.

FIELD OF HYACINTHS.
Grown by
J. W. CROSS, WISBECH.

BULB CULTIVATION was at its height towards the end of the last century when the hyacinth was at the peak of its popularity. Many new varieties were introduced and the principal buyers were the large corporations who needed them for civic bedding schemes. To cater for the demand many nurseries turned over whole fields to the cultivation of hyacinths, as did J W Cross of Wisbech.

SEABIRDS were the source of a manure so in demand by nineteenth century gardeners that whole ships were taken over for its transportation. Along the coastline of South America the birds deposited mountains of guano and it proved to be so rich in nutrients that double pickings could be expected from any crop to which it was applied. When supplies ran out canary guano was substituted. It sold for a shilling a tin.